Table of Contents

Introduction

Extra practice is often the key to better accuracy and speed when working math problems. Learners can build confidence and ability as they review the skills necessary to understand a math concept and then apply those skills in a series of practice exercises. The **Head for Home Math** series provides additional practice with math skills for learners at all ability levels.

Head for Home Math: Grade 4 Novice is designed to help struggling learners build and improve their understanding of math concepts. The Novice level for Grade 4 includes ten lessons that target key math skills. Each Novice lesson includes the following:

- An introduction explains the skill in student-friendly language and provides clear, step-by-step instructions that walk students through example problems.

- Multiple-choice and open-ended exercises allow students multiple opportunities to practice the skill.

By choosing this workbook, you are helping your child build a better understanding of math concepts. Thank you for being involved in your child's learning. Here are a few suggestions for helping your child with math concepts.

- Read the instructions for each skill with your child and discuss the concepts.

- Practice math skills while riding in the car, shopping, or preparing meals. Help your child discover that math applies to everyday life.

- Check the lesson when it is complete. Note areas of improvement and praise your child for success. Also note areas of concern and provide additional support as necessary.

Skill Focus:
Associative Property of Multiplication

Objective: To use the Associative Property of Multiplication to solve multiplication problems

Multiplication is the process of finding the total number of items in equal-sized groups, or finding the total number of items in a given number of groups when each group contains the same number of items.

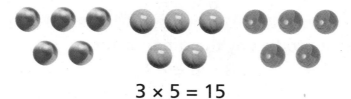

$$3 \times 5 = 15$$

A **factor** is a number that is multiplied by another number to find a product. The factors in the problem below are 4 and 7.

$$\begin{array}{r} 4 \\ \times 7 \\ \hline 28 \end{array} \quad \text{factors}$$

A **product** is the answer to a multiplication problem. The product in the problem below is 28.

$$\begin{array}{r} 4 \\ \times 7 \\ \hline 28 \end{array} \quad \longleftarrow \text{product}$$

The **Associative Property of Multiplication** is also known as the grouping property. It states that you can group factors in different ways and still get the same product.

$$(4 \times 2) \times 3 = ? \qquad\qquad 4 \times (2 \times 3) = ?$$

$$8 \times 3 = 24 \qquad\qquad 4 \times 6 = 24$$

The Associative Property of Multiplication shows that you can group numbers any way you want to multiply and you will get the same answer. So if you have three factors, you can group them in whichever way is easiest for you.

Use the Associative Property to multiply 2, 4, and 6.

Step 1: Multiply the factors in parenthesis.
$$(2 \times 4) \times 6 = ?$$
$$8 \times 6 = ?$$

Step 2: Multiply that product by the other factor.
$$8 \times 6 = 48$$

Step 3: Now, regroup the factors. Multiply the factors in the parenthesis.
$$2 \times (4 \times 6) = ?$$
$$2 \times 24 = ?$$

Step 4: Multiply that product by the other factor.
$$2 \times 24 = 48$$

Step 5: Compare. Both products should be the same.
$$48 = 48$$

Example 1:

$(5 \times 2) \times 4 = ?$ $5 \times (2 \times 4) = ?$

$10 \times 4 = 40$ $5 \times 8 = $ _____

Example 2:

$(2 \times 3) \times 5 = ?$ $2 \times (3 \times 5) = ?$

_____ $\times 5 = $ _____ $2 \times$ _____ $= $ _____

Multiplying Using the Associative Property

Directions: Read each problem carefully. Circle the letter of the correct answer. For the open-ended items, write or draw your answer in the space provided.

1 Which number belongs in the box to make the number sentence correct?

$$4 \times (7 \times 3) = (\boxed{} \times 7) \times 3$$

A. 3

B. 4

C. 6

D. 10

2 Which number belongs in the box to make the number sentence correct?

$$\boxed{} \times (9 \times 4) = (3 \times 9) \times 4$$

A. 3

B. 4

C. 7

D. 9

3 Which shows another way to get the same product?

$$(6 \times 2) \times 4 = 48$$

A. $6 \times (2 + 4)$

B. $6 + (2 \times 4)$

C. $6 \times (2 \times 6)$

D. $6 \times (2 \times 4)$

4 Write another way to group the factors in $(3 \times 5) \times 4$.

$$(4 \times 5) \times 3$$

5 Which shows another way to get the same product?

$$5 \times (8 \times 3) = 120$$

A. $(5 \times 8) + 3$
B. $(5 \times 8) \times 2$
C. $(5 \times 8) \times 3$
D. $(5 + 8) \times 3$

6 Which expression is equivalent to $(2 \times 7) \times 5$?

A. $(2 \times 7) + (2 \times 5)$
B. $(2 \times 7) \times (2 \times 5)$
C. $2 \times (7 \times 5)$
D. $(2 \times 7) + 5$

7 Which number belongs in the box to make the number sentence correct?

$$(7 \times 2) \times 5 = \boxed{7} \times (2 \times 5)$$

A. 2
B. 5
C. 6
D. 7

8 Which expression is equivalent to $4 \times (9 \times 8)$?

A. $(9 \times 4) + 8$
B. $(9 \times 4) \times 4$
C. $(9 \times 4) \times 8$
D. $(9 \times 4) \times (8 \times 4)$

9 Which equation shows the Associative Property of Multiplication?

    A. $(3 \times 4) = (3 \times 4)$

    B. $(3 \times 4) = (4 \times 3)$

    C. $(3 \times 4) \times 5 = 3 \times (4 \times 5)$

    D. $(3 \times 4) + 5 = (3 \times 5) + (4 \times 5)$

10 Carlos wrote the number sentence shown below. Which number belongs in the box?

$$(5 \times \square) \times 7 = 5 \times (8 \times 7)$$

    A. 8

    B. 7

    C. 6

    D. 5

11 Meaghan found the number sentence below in her math book.

$$2 \times (5 \times 12) = (2 \times 5) \times 12 = 120$$

Which property of multiplication was used to find the product?

    A. Commutative Property of Multiplication

    B. Associative Property of Multiplication

    C. Identity Property of Multiplication

    D. Zero Property

12 Andrew wants to show the Associative Property of Multiplication. He wrote the following equations.

$$(3 \times 4) \times 5 = (3 \times 4) + 5$$

What mistakes did Andrew make? Explain.

He did (3x4) +5 instead
of doubling (3x4) x 5.

13 David puts 2 stacks of 6 plates on 5 tables. He says to find out how many plates in all, multiply 2 × 5 and then multiply that product by 6. Anita says, multiply 5 × 6 and then multiply that product by 2 to get the total number of plates.

Whose method will get the correct number of plates? Explain.

_____

_____

_____

_____

_____

_____

_____

14 Amy wrote the number sentence shown below.

$$(6 \times \boxed{}) \times 3 = 6 \times (4 \times 3)$$

Write the number that belongs in the box to make the number sentence correct.

_____

15 Use the Associative Property of Multiplication to complete the number sentence below.

$(4 \times 9) \times 2 =$ _____

Skill Focus: Remainders

Objective: To solve division problems with remainders

Sometimes you cannot divide objects evenly into groups.
Find $14 \div 4$.

Use 14 counters.

Divide the 14 counters into 4 equal groups by putting them, one at a time, into each group until you don't have enough left to put one in each group.

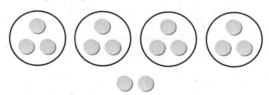

The **quotient** is 3—the number of counters in each of the 4 groups.

The **remainder** is 2—the number of leftover counters. So, $14 \div 4 = 3$ r2.

Finding Remainders Other Ways

Think: If you divide 23 into 5 equal groups, how many are in each group?

$$5 \times ? = 23$$

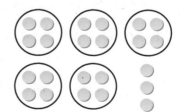

There are 5 groups of 4, with 3 left over.

Think: How many groups of 5 can you make from 23?

$$? \times 5 = 23$$

There are 4 groups of 5, with 3 left over.

Remainders
Head for Home Math, Grade 4

Two different ways to think about 23 ÷ 5 are shown below.

23 ÷ 5 = 4 r3

$$\begin{array}{r} 4\text{ r}3 \\ 5\overline{)23} \\ -20 \\ \hline 3 \end{array}$$

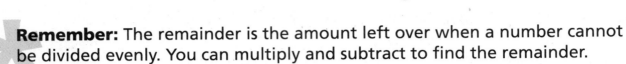

Remember: The remainder is the amount left over when a number cannot be divided evenly. You can multiply and subtract to find the remainder.

Dividing Using Facts

Facts of 2	Facts of 3	Facts of 4	Facts of 5	Facts of 6
18 ÷ 2 = 9	27 ÷ 3 = 9	36 ÷ 4 = 9	45 ÷ 5 = 9	54 ÷ 6 = 9
16 ÷ 2 = 8	24 ÷ 3 = 8	32 ÷ 4 = 8	40 ÷ 5 = 8	48 ÷ 6 = 8
14 ÷ 2 = 7	21 ÷ 3 = 7	28 ÷ 4 = 7	35 ÷ 5 = 7	42 ÷ 6 = 7
12 ÷ 2 = 6	18 ÷ 3 = 6	24 ÷ 4 = 6	30 ÷ 5 = 6	36 ÷ 6 = 6
10 ÷ 2 = 5	15 ÷ 3 = 5	20 ÷ 4 = 5	25 ÷ 5 = 5	30 ÷ 6 = 5
8 ÷ 2 = 4	12 ÷ 3 = 4	16 ÷ 4 = 4	20 ÷ 5 = 4	24 ÷ 6 = 4
6 ÷ 2 = 3	9 ÷ 3 = 3	12 ÷ 4 = 3	15 ÷ 5 = 3	18 ÷ 6 = 3
4 ÷ 2 = 2	6 ÷ 3 = 2	8 ÷ 4 = 2	10 ÷ 5 = 2	12 ÷ 6 = 2
2 ÷ 2 = 1	3 ÷ 3 = 1	4 ÷ 4 = 1	5 ÷ 5 = 1	6 ÷ 6 = 1

How can you find 23 ÷ 5 using facts?

Step 1: Find the fact whose dividend is closest to, yet less than, the dividend in the problem.

The fact closest to 23 ÷ 5 is <u>20 ÷ 5</u>.

Step 2: Subtract the dividends to find your remainder.

23 − 20 = 3

So, 23 ÷ 5 = 4 r3

Example: What is 33 ÷ 5?

Closest fact: 30 ÷ 5 = 6

Subtract: _____

So, 33 ÷ 5 = _____

Dividing with Remainders

Directions: Read each problem carefully. Circle the letter of the correct answer. For the open-ended items, write or draw your answer in the space provided.

1 Use the picture to find the quotient and remainder.

$$9 \div 4 = \underline{\hspace{2cm}}$$

   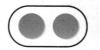

2 Find the quotient. Find how many are left.

What is the quotient? _____

How many are left? _____

$$5 \div 2 = \underline{\hspace{3cm}}$$

3 Draw a picture to find the quotient and remainder.

$$13 \div 6 = \underline{\hspace{2cm}}$$

4 Find the quotient. Find how many are left.

What is the quotient? _____

How many are left? _____

14 ÷ 4 = _____

5 3)‾28‾

A. 9
B. 9 r1
C. 8 r1
D. 8 r4

6 Solve.

23 ÷ 6

Closest fact: _____

Subtract: _____

23 ÷ 6 = _____

7 $8\overline{)35}$

    A. 3 r5

    B. 3 r4

    C. 4 r3

    D. 5 r5

8 $7\overline{)58}$

    A. 8 r2

    B. 8 r3

    C. 9 r3

    D. 9 r3

9 Which fact would you use to solve $17 \div 3$?

    A. $16 \div 2 = 8$

    B. $18 \div 2 = 9$

    C. $21 \div 3 = 7$

    D. $15 \div 3 = 5$

10 Michael wants to use $24 \div 4 = 6$ to solve $22 \div 4$.
What mistake did he make? Which fact should he use?

_____

_____

_____

_____

_____

11 Which fact would you use to solve 19 ÷ 2?

    A. 20 ÷ 4 = 5

    B. 25 ÷ 5 = 5

    C. 24 ÷ 4 = 6

    D. 18 ÷ 2 = 9

12 Solve. $5\overline{)32}$

13 Solve. $3\overline{)22}$

14 Solve. $6\overline{)19}$

Skill Focus:
Numbers and Place Value

Objective: To read and write numbers from one to 10,000 and explain place value for 4-digit numbers

A **digit** is any one of ten symbols used to write numerals.

0, 1, 2, 3, 4, 5, 6, 7, 8, or 9

Place value is the value of the digits in a number.

234 = 2 hundreds, 3 tens, and 4 ones

A **place-value chart** can be used to show the value of a digit's place in a number.

	Thousands	Hundreds	Tens	Ones
2,634 =	2,	6	3	4

Standard form is a way to write numbers by using digits: *2,635.*

Reading and Writing Numbers

Numbers are read in words according to the place value of the digits.

Example 1: 7,208

Thousands	Hundreds	Tens	Ones
7,	2	0	8

Words: seven thousand, two hundred eight

Example 2: 9,432

Thousands	Hundreds	Tens	Ones

Words: _____

Writing Numbers

Numbers can be written in standard form or words.

	Standard Form	Words
Example 3:	1,934	one thousand, nine hundred thirty-four
Example 4:		seven thousand, sixty-two
Example 5:	4,107	

For 2-digit number words greater than 20, add a hyphen between the two words.

34 is written thirty-four.

76 is written seventy-six.

Zeros do not need to be written in words.

2,006 is written two thousand, six.

408 is written four hundred eight.

In order to explain place value, you must determine and explain the value of each digit in the number. We can use a place-value chart to help us determine these values.

	Thousands	Hundreds	Tens	Ones
1,972 =	1,	9	7	2
3,051 =	3,	0	5	1
9,500 =	9,	5	0	0

Example 1: Explain the place value of the digits in the number 1,972.

       1 thousand
       9 hundreds
       7 tens
       2 ones

Example 2: Explain the place value of the digits in the number 3,051.

    _____ thousands

    _____ tens

    _____ ones

Example 3: Explain the place value of the digits in the number 9,500.

    _____

    _____

Writing Numbers and Determining Values

Directions: Read each problem carefully. Circle the letter of the correct answer. For the open-ended items, write or draw your answer in the space provided.

1 What is the value of the underlined digit in the number below?

6,<u>4</u>13

A. 4

B. 40

C. 400

D. 4,000

2 Which of the following represents the number seven thousand, seven in standard form?

A. 7,770

B. 7,070

C. 7,017

D. 7,007

3 Which digit in the number below is in the tens place?

2,386

A. 2

B. 3

C. 8

D. 6

4 How many thousands are in the number below?

4,891

_____ thousands

5 Samuel correctly read the number 3,002 in words. Which of the following shows what Samuel said?

A. three thousand, two

B. three thousand, zero zero two

C. three thousand, twenty

D. three thousand, two hundred

6 In which place is the underlined digit in the number below?

7,42<u>6</u>

A. ones

B. tens

C. hundreds

D. thousands

7 Nicole correctly wrote the number four thousand nineteen in standard form. Which of the following shows what Nicole wrote?

A. 4,000 and 19

B. 4,000 + 19

C. 4,009

D. 4,019

8 Which of the following explains the place value of each digit in the number 4,317?

    A. 4 thousands, 3 hundreds, 17 ones
    B. 4 thousands, 3 hundreds, 1 ten, 7 ones
    C. 4 thousands, 31 tens, 7 ones
    D. four thousand, three hundred seventeen

9 Write the following number in standard form.

        eight thousand, seven

_____

10 Kaitlyn correctly wrote a number in standard form to represent the words nine thousand, three hundred sixty-four. Which of the following numbers did Kaitlyn write?

    A. 9,463
    B. 9,364
    C. 9,360
    D. 9,304

11 Explain the place value of the digits in the number 6,012.

_____

_____

_____

12 Write the number 9,408 in words.

_____

_____

Skill Focus: Adding Fractions

Objective: To add fractions with like denominators

A **fraction** is a number that names part of a whole or part of a group.

$\frac{1}{2}$ $\frac{1}{2}$

The **numerator** is the number above the line. It tells how many parts of the whole are being considered. The **denominator** is the number below the line. It tells how many equal parts are in the whole.

$\frac{4}{5}$ ← —————— numerator

———— denominator

A fraction is written in its **simplest form** when 1 is the only number that can divided evenly in both the numerator and denominator.

| $\frac{1}{4}$ | $\frac{1}{4}$ | $\frac{2}{4}$ |

| $\frac{1}{2}$ | $\frac{1}{2}$ |

$\frac{2}{4}$ in simplest form is $\frac{1}{2}$

Adding Fractions with Like Denominators

You can use drawings to add fractions with like denominators.

Find $\frac{3}{8} + \frac{4}{8}$.

Step 1: Use a shape that is divided equally into the number of sections that matches the denominator.

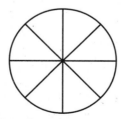

Adding Fractions
Head for Home Math, Grade 4

Step 2: Color the number of parts to match the numerator of the first fraction.

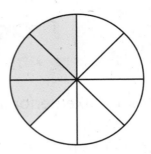

Step 3: Color the number of parts to match the numerator of the second fraction.

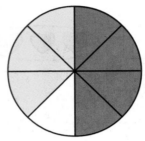

Step 4: Count how many parts are shaded.

$$\frac{3}{8} + \frac{4}{8} = \frac{7}{8}$$

Another way to add fractions with like denominators is to add the numerators. The denominator stays the same.

Find $\frac{2}{6} + \frac{2}{6}$.

Step 1: Add the numerators.

$$\frac{2}{6} + \frac{2}{6} = \frac{4}{\boxed{}}$$

Step 2: Write the denominator. Remember, the denominator stays the same.

$$\frac{2}{6} + \frac{2}{6} = \frac{4}{6}$$

Step 3: Reduce to simplest form if necessary.

$$\frac{4}{6} = \frac{4 \div 2}{6 \div 2} = \frac{2}{3}.$$

So, $\frac{2}{6} + \frac{2}{6} = \frac{2}{3}$.

A **mixed number** is a whole number and a fraction. When adding mixed numbers, first add the fractions and then add the whole numbers.

Find $7\frac{2}{6} + 4\frac{2}{6}$.

Step 1:
Add the fractions.

$$7\frac{2}{6}$$
$$+4\frac{2}{6}$$
$$\overline{\quad\frac{4}{6}}$$

Step 2:
Add the whole numbers.

$$7\frac{2}{6}$$
$$+4\frac{2}{6}$$
$$\overline{11\frac{4}{6}}$$

Step 3:
Reduce to simplest form.

$$7\frac{2}{6}$$
$$+4\frac{2}{6}$$
$$\overline{11\frac{4}{6} = 11\frac{2}{3}}$$

So, the sum is $11\frac{2}{3}$.

Example 1:

$$5\frac{3}{10}$$
$$+\ \frac{6}{10}$$
$$\overline{5\frac{9}{10}}$$

Example 2:

$$5\frac{2}{9}$$
$$+2\frac{4}{9}$$
$$\overline{7\frac{6}{9}} = \underline{\quad\quad}$$

Example 3:

$$3\frac{4}{7}$$
$$+2\frac{3}{7}$$
$$\overline{\quad\quad}$$

Adding Fractions and Mixed Numbers

Directions: Read each problem carefully. Circle the letter of the correct answer. For the open-ended items, write or draw your answer in the space provided.

1 Use the model to help you add.

$\frac{2}{10} + \frac{5}{10} = $ _____

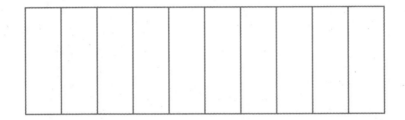

2 Add. Show how you add the numerators. Reduce to simplest form.

$\frac{1}{9} + \frac{2}{9} = $

3 Add.

$\frac{2}{5} + \frac{2}{5} = $

A. $\frac{4}{10}$

B. $\frac{5}{4}$

C. $\frac{4}{5}$

D. $\frac{2}{10}$

4 Add.

$$\frac{2}{7} + \frac{3}{7} =$$

A. $\frac{4}{7}$ B. $\frac{5}{7}$

C. $\frac{7}{5}$ D. $\frac{5}{14}$

5 Add. Reduce to simplest form.

$$\frac{2}{8} + \frac{4}{8} =$$

A. $\frac{6}{8}$ B. $\frac{6}{16}$

C. $\frac{3}{4}$ D. $\frac{1}{2}$

Adding Mixed Numbers

Directions: Read each problem carefully. Circle the letter of the correct answer. For the open-ended items, write or draw your answer in the space provided.

For Items 6–9, add. Reduce to simplest form.

6 $6\frac{1}{4} + \frac{2}{4} =$

A. $\frac{3}{4}$ B. $6\frac{3}{8}$

C. $6\frac{1}{2}$ D. $6\frac{3}{4}$

7 $5\frac{3}{8} + 4\frac{2}{8} =$

    A. $9\frac{5}{8}$ **B.** $9\frac{5}{16}$

    C. $9\frac{1}{4}$ **D.** 10

8 $1\frac{2}{5} + \frac{3}{5} =$

    A. $1\frac{5}{5}$ **B.** $1\frac{5}{10}$

    C. $1\frac{1}{2}$ **D.** 2

9 $8\frac{1}{7} + 4\frac{4}{7} =$

    A. $11\frac{5}{7}$ **B.** $12\frac{5}{14}$

    C. $12\frac{5}{7}$ **D.** $12\frac{3}{7}$

10 Add. Reduce to simplest form.

    $3\frac{1}{10} + 6\frac{3}{10} =$

Skill Focus: Subtracting Fractions

Objective: To subtract fractions with like denominators

Subtracting Fractions with Like Denominators

You can use drawings to help you subtract fractions with like denominators.

Find: $\frac{5}{7} - \frac{3}{7}$.

Step 1: Use a shape with the same number of sections that matches the denominator. Then, shade the number of parts matching the numerator of the first number.

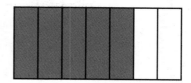

Step 2: Draw an X on the number of parts matching the numerator of the fraction you are subtracting.

Step 3: Count the number of shaded parts that are left.

So, $\frac{5}{7} - \frac{3}{7} = \frac{2}{7}$.

When you subtract like fractions, you only subtract the numerators. The denominator stays the same.

Find: $\frac{6}{8} - \frac{2}{8}$.

Step 1: Subtract the numerators. $\frac{6}{8} - \frac{2}{8} = \frac{4}{\Box}$

Step 2: Write in the denominator. $\frac{6}{8} - \frac{2}{8} = \frac{4}{8}$

Step 3: Reduce the fraction to simplest form. $\frac{4}{8} = \frac{4 \div 4}{8 \div 4} = \frac{1}{2}$

So, $\frac{6}{8} - \frac{2}{8} = \frac{1}{2}$.

When subtracting mixed numbers, first subtract the fractions and then subtract the whole numbers.

Find $8\frac{5}{6} - 1\frac{3}{6}$.

Step 1:
Subtract the fractions.

$$\begin{array}{r} 8\frac{5}{6} \\ -1\frac{3}{6} \\ \hline \frac{2}{6} \end{array}$$

Step 2:
Subtract the whole numbers.

$$\begin{array}{r} 8\frac{5}{6} \\ -1\frac{3}{6} \\ \hline 7\frac{2}{6} \end{array}$$

Step 3:
Reduce to simplest form.

$$\begin{array}{r} 8\frac{5}{6} \\ -1\frac{3}{6} \\ \hline 7\frac{2}{6} = 7\frac{1}{3} \end{array}$$

So, the difference is $7\frac{1}{3}$.

Example 1:

$$\begin{array}{r} 5\frac{6}{10} \\ -\ \frac{3}{10} \\ \hline 5\frac{3}{10} \end{array}$$

Example 2:

$$\begin{array}{r} 7\frac{8}{10} \\ -4\frac{6}{10} \\ \hline 3\frac{2}{10} = \end{array}$$

Example 3:

$$\begin{array}{r} 3\frac{6}{9} \\ -2\frac{5}{9} \\ \hline \end{array}$$

Subtracting Fractions

Directions: Read each problem carefully. Circle the letter of the correct answer. For the open-ended items, write or draw your answer in the space provided.

1 Cross out the correct number of parts. Then, complete.

$$\frac{5}{6} - \frac{3}{6} = \underline{\hspace{1cm}}$$

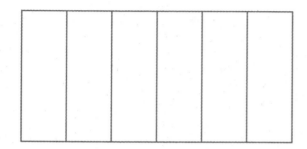

2 Subtract. Show how you subtract the numerators. Reduce to simplest form.

$$\frac{8}{10} - \frac{3}{10} =$$

3 Subtract.

$$\frac{7}{8} - \frac{4}{8} =$$

A. $\frac{11}{8}$ **B.** $\frac{3}{8}$

C. $\frac{3}{0}$ **D.** 3

4 Subtract.

$$\frac{6}{7} - \frac{3}{7} =$$

A. $\frac{3}{7}$

B. $\frac{9}{7}$

C. $\frac{1}{2}$

D. $\frac{1}{3}$

5 Subtract. Reduce to simplest form.

$$\frac{6}{8} - \frac{4}{8} =$$

A. $\frac{2}{8}$

B. $\frac{1}{8}$

C. $\frac{1}{2}$

D. $\frac{1}{4}$

6 Subtract. Reduce to simplest form.

$$\frac{4}{5} - \frac{1}{5} =$$

A. $\frac{5}{5}$

B. $\frac{3}{10}$

C. $\frac{2}{5}$

D. $\frac{3}{5}$

Subtracting Mixed Numbers

Directions: Read each problem carefully. Circle the letter of the correct answer. For the open-ended items, write or draw your answer in the space provided.

For items 7–10, subtract. Reduce to simplest form.

7 $4\frac{5}{6} - 3\frac{3}{6} =$

   A. $7\frac{1}{3}$

   B. $1\frac{1}{3}$

   C. $1\frac{2}{6}$

   D. $1\frac{1}{2}$

8 $7\frac{8}{9} - 6 =$

   A. $13\frac{8}{9}$

   B. $1\frac{2}{9}$

   C. $1\frac{8}{9}$

   D. $\frac{8}{9}$

9 $9\frac{9}{10} - 5\frac{2}{10} =$

    A. $4\frac{7}{10}$

    B. $4\frac{11}{10}$

    C. $3\frac{7}{10}$

    D. $4\frac{6}{10}$

10 $8\frac{2}{4} - 6\frac{1}{4} =$

    A. $2\frac{3}{4}$

    B. $2\frac{1}{2}$

    C. $2\frac{1}{4}$

    D. $1\frac{3}{4}$

11 Subtract. Reduce to simplest form.

$3\frac{10}{12} - 1\frac{7}{12} =$

Skill Focus: Decimals

Objective: To model, read, and write decimal numbers through thousandths

Reading and Writing Decimal Numbers

A **decimal** is a number that uses place value and a decimal point to show values that are less than one. Write whole numbers to the left of the **decimal point.** Write decimals to the right of the decimal point.

$$6.932$$

decimal point ⟶

You can use a place-value chart to find the value of each digit in a decimal.

ones	decimal point	tenths	hundredths	thousandths
6	.	9	3	2

You can write a decimal in standard form and with words. When you write a decimal with words, use *and* for the decimal point.

Standard form: 6.932

Words: six and nine hundred thirty-two thousandths

When you read a decimal, start with the whole numbers. Then, read *and* for the decimal point. Then read the decimal numbers.

Decimal	Read as
9.9	nine and nine tenths
9.09	nine and nine hundredths
9.009	nine and nine thousandths

Decimals
Head for Home Math, Grade 4

You can use models to show decimals.

Model 0.6.

Step 1: Draw a shape with ten equal sections. Each section represents one tenth.

Step 2: Shade in the amount to show the decimal.

.6 is 6 tenths. So, shade in 6 sections.

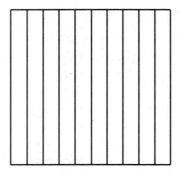

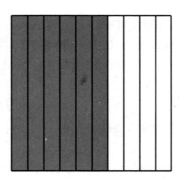

Model .60.

Step 1: Draw a shape with 100 equal sections. Each section represents one hundredth.

Step 2: Shade in the amount to show the decimal.

.60 is 60 hundredths. So, shade in 60 sections.

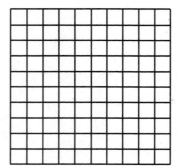

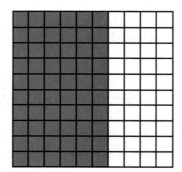

Practicing Decimal Number Place Value

Directions: Read each problem carefully. Circle the letter of the correct answer. For the open-ended items, write or draw your answer in the space provided.

For items 1–3, read the decimal number, paying attention to the place value of each digit. Then create a model to represent it.

1 0.25

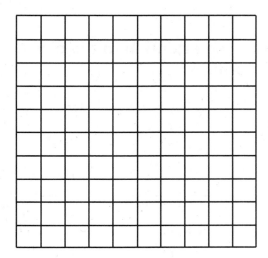

2 0.09

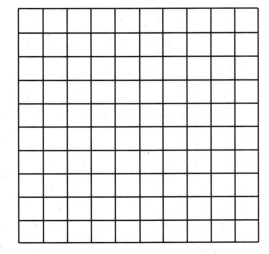

Decimals
Head for Home Math, Grade 4

3 0.8

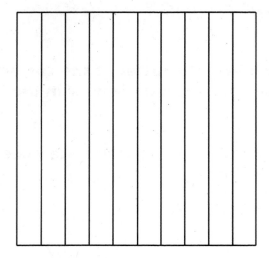

For items 4–6, read the decimal number, paying attention to the place value of each digit. Then write it in word form.

4 0.678

word form: _____

5 0.32

word form: _____

6 0.80

word form: _____

7 Each small square represent 0.01. Which number equals the shaded region of the grid below?

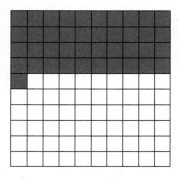

A. 0.04

B. 0.05

C. 0.41

D. 4.1

8 Which of the following correctly represents 5 thousandths?

A. 5,000

B. 0.500

C. 0.05

D. 0.005

9 Which of the following correctly represents four and thirty-two hundredths?

A. 4.032

B. 4.32

C. 43.200

D. 0.432

10 Each small rectangle represents 0.1 of the figure below. Which number equals the shaded region of the figure?

A. 0.04

B. 0.06

C. 0.6

D. 4.0

11 How would you represent 0.641 in word form?

A. six tenths and forty-one hundredths

B. six hundred forty-one tenths

C. six hundred forty-one hundredths

D. six hundred forty-one thousandths

12 What is the word form of the decimal below?

9.41

A. nine and forty-one hundredths

B. nine and forty-one thousandths

C. nine and forty-one tenths

D. nine hundred forty-one hundredths

Skill Focus: Number Patterns

Objective: To use patterns to make generalizations and predictions by determining a rule and identifying missing numbers in a sequence

Determining a Pattern Rule

A **pattern** is a series of figures or numbers that is repeated.
A **pattern rule** governs a pattern, such as add 2 or subtract 5.

Step 1: Determine how the first two numbers relate to each other.

$$\overset{+2}{}$$
2, 4, 6, 8, _____

Step 2: Determine how the second and third numbers relate to each other.

$$+2 \ +2$$
2, 4, 6, 8, _____

Step 3: Continue to determine how each 2 numbers next to each other relate.

$$+2 \ +2 \ +2$$
2, 4, 6, 8, _____

Step 4: Name the pattern rule.

$$+2 \ +2 \ +2$$
2, 4, 6, 8, _____

The pattern rule is add 2.

Step 5: Apply the rule and write the number that would come next.

2, 4, 6, 8, _10_

Think: Which operation(s) is used?

$$-4 \ -4 \ -4$$
Example 1: 24, 20, 16, 12, _____   Pattern rule: subtract 4

$$\times 2 \ \times 2 \ \times 2 \ \times 2$$
Example 2: 1, 2, 4, 8, 16, _____   Pattern rule: _____

Step 1: Identify the pattern rule.

$$\overset{+3}{}\quad\overset{+3}{}\quad\overset{+3}{}\quad\overset{+3}{}\quad\overset{+3}{}\quad\overset{+3}{}$$

305, 308, 311, _____ , 317, _____ , 323.

The pattern rule is add 3.

Step 2: Apply the rule to find the missing numbers.

$$311 + 3 = 314$$
$$317 + 3 = 320$$

So, the missing numbers are 314 and 320.

Step 3: Fill in the numbers and check to see if the pattern rule works.

305, 308, 311, 314, 317, 320, 323

Think: Which operation is used?

Example: 36, 30, _____ , 18, 12, _____

It is important to look at how each number relates to the one next to it. Sometimes a pattern can use more than one operation.

$$\overset{-10}{}\quad\overset{+5}{}\quad\overset{-10}{}\quad\overset{+5}{}\quad\overset{-10}{}\quad\overset{+5}{}$$

50, 40, 45, 35, 40, 30, 35.

The pattern here uses both subtraction and addition. The pattern rule is subtract 10, add 5.

Using Patterns

Directions: Read each problem carefully. Circle the letter of the correct answer. For the open-ended items, write or draw your answer in the space provided.

1 What is the rule for this pattern?

562, 570, 578, 586, 594, 602

A. Add 7.

B. Subtract 7.

C. Add 8.

D. Subtract 8.

2 What is the rule for this pattern?

591, 594, 597, 600, 603, 606, 609

A. Add 3.

B. Subtract 3.

C. Add 3, subtract 2.

D. Add 4.

3 What is the rule for this pattern?

606, 600, 602, 596, 598, 592, 594

A. Subtract 6.

B. Subtract 3.

C. Subtract 6, add 2.

D. Subtract 6, add 3.

4 What number is missing from this pattern?

125, 130, _____ , 140, 145

A. 100

B. 120

C. 131

D. 135

5 What number is missing from this pattern?

427, _____ , 431, 433, 435

A. 432

B. 429

C. 428

D. 425

6 What number is missing from this pattern?

970, 965, 960, _____ , 950

A. 955

B. 961

C. 963

D. 965

7 What are the next three numbers in this pattern?

81, 72, 63, 54, _____ , _____ , _____

A. 45, 36, 27

B. 27, 36, 45

C. 36, 45, 54

D. 54, 36, 18

8 What number is missing from this pattern?

618, 610, _____ , 594, 586

A. 620
B. 612
C. 602
D. 601

9 Write the next number and the rule for this pattern.

22, 24, 26, 28, 30, 32, _____

_____

10 Write the next number and the rule for this pattern.

21, 18, 15, 12, 9, 6, _____

_____

11 Write the next number and the rule for this pattern.

35, 40, 39, 44, 43, 48, _____

_____

12 Find the pattern rule. Then find the missing numbers.

6, 12, 11, 17, _____ , 22, 21, _____ , 26

_____   _____

Skill Focus: Equations

Objective: To understand equivalence is the foundation of mathematics represented in equations

Understanding Equations

Equations are number sentences that include symbols, such as letters, which are called **variables.** Variables represent an unknown part of the problem. The key words in a problem can tell us which operations to use in the equation.

Key Words	Operation
altogether, in all, add, more, total	addition
subtract, difference, less than, more than	subtraction
product, each, multiply	multiplication
divides, quotient, each	division

Ted's dad has 43 nails in a jar. He adds 29 more nails to the jar. How many nails are there altogether?

Step 1: Look for key words.

The key words are *more* and *altogether.*

Step 2: Determine the operation to be used.

We need to *add* to solve.

Step 3: Determine the unknown. Choose a letter to represent the unknown.

The total number of nails is unknown. We can use *n* to represent the nails.

Step 4: Write the equation and solve.

$$43 + 29 = n$$
$$43 + 29 = 72$$

So, $n = 72$.

Addition and subtraction are **inverse operations.** That means they will "undo" each other. If you are trying to undo addition to find the missing value in an equation, you use subtraction. If you are trying to undo subtraction, you use addition.

Find $x - 4 = 10$.

Step 1: Think: What is being done to x?

4 is being subtracted from x.

What is the inverse operation of subtraction? <u>addition</u>

Step 2: Add 4 to both sides.

$$\begin{array}{r} x - 4 = 10 \\ +4 \quad +4 \\ \hline x \quad\;\; = 14 \end{array}$$

Step 3: Check.

$$\begin{array}{r} x - 4 = 10 \\ (14) - 4 = 10 \\ 10 = 10 \end{array}$$

Multiplication and division are also inverse operations. If you are trying to undo multiplication, you use division. If you are trying to undo division, you use multiplication.

Find $24 = 3 \times s$.

Step 1: Think: What is being done to s?

It is multiplied by 3.

What is the inverse operation of multiplication? <u>division</u>

Step 2: Divide each side by 3.

$$\frac{24}{3} = \frac{3s}{3}$$
$$8 = s$$

Step 3: Check.

$$24 = 3s$$
$$24 = 3(8)$$
$$24 = 24$$

Working with Equations

Directions: Read each problem carefully. Circle the letter of the correct answer. For the open-ended items, write or draw your answer in the space provided.

1 Kevin has some trading cards. After he traded 4 of his cards, he had 20 left. How many trading cards did Kevin begin with?

$c - 4 = 20$

A. 16
B. 20
C. 22
D. 24

2 Solve for n.

$7 + n = 36$

A. 43
B. 36
C. 29
D. 28

3 Solve for n.

$n \div 5 = 7$

A. 35
B. 40
C. 45
D. 50

4 Tanya used 34 beads to make a bracelet. She has 23 beads left. How many beads did Tanya have before she made the bracelet? Write an equation.

5 Connor owns a toy car collection. Next week, he will buy 3 more cars, for a total of 15 cars. How many cars does Connor own now?

$3 + n = 15$

A. 18
B. 12
C. 10
D. 3

6 Solve for n.

$7 + n = 28$

A. 7
B. 12
C. 21
D. 35

7 Solve for j. Show your work.

$j - 13 = 27$

8 In Maria's pantry, there are 4 shelves. There are a total of 44 items in the pantry. Using the simple equation below, solve to find out how many items are on each shelf if each shelf has an equal number of items. Show your work.

$n \times 4 = 44$

9 Mrs. Henderson spent a total of 54 dollars on pizzas for a class party. Each pizza cost 6 dollars. How many pizzas did Mrs. Henderson buy altogether?

$6 \times p = 54$

A. 6

B. 9

C. 48

D. 60

10 Ricky ran 12 miles more than Mike, which was a total of 20 miles. How many miles did Mike run?

$m + 12 = 20$

A. 8

B. 12

C. 20

D. 32

11 Solve for n.

$n \div 12 = 4$

A. 3

B. 8

C. 16

D. 48

12 Write an equation that represents the situation below and solve, showing all work.

Del had some candy. He gave away 13 pieces. He had 23 pieces left.

Skill Focus: Rounding Numbers

Objective: To round numbers to the tens place to determine if the estimated sums, differences, or products are greater than or less than the exact sum or difference

Rounding to the Nearest Ten

Rounding to the nearest ten is finding a number that is close to a number in the tens place. We can round numbers to the nearest ten to **estimate,** or make a guess, to solve a problem.

To round a number to the nearest ten, look at the digit in the ones place. If the digit in the ones place is 5 or greater, round the number to the next tens number. This is called rounding up.

Example 1: 56 would round up to 60 because the number in the ones place is greater than 5.

rounds to

5**6** ⟶ 60

If the digit in the ones place of the number you want to round is less than 5, the digit in the tens place stays the same.

Example 2: 53 would round to 50. The 5 in the tens place stays the same because the number in the ones place is less than 5.

rounds to

5**3** ⟶ 50

Sometimes you need to find the **exact answer,** or actual answer, to a problem. Other times, you only need to find an **estimate,** or a very close guess.

Step 1: Add, subtract, or multiply to find the exact answer.

$$\begin{array}{r} 13 \\ 73 \\ + 56 \\ \hline 142 \end{array}$$

Step 2: Round numbers to the nearest ten and find the estimated answer.

$$\begin{array}{r} 10 \\ 70 \\ + 60 \\ \hline 140 \end{array}$$

Step 3: Compare to see if the estimated answer is *greater than* or *less than* the exact answer.

142 > 140. The estimated sum is *less than* the exact sum.

Example 1:

Exact difference

$$\begin{array}{r} 46 \\ - 12 \\ \hline \mathbf{34} \end{array}$$

Estimated difference

$$\begin{array}{r} 50 \\ - 10 \\ \hline \mathbf{40} \end{array}$$

The estimated difference is _____ the exact difference.

Example 2:

Exact product

$$\begin{array}{r} 16 \\ \times 5 \\ \hline \end{array}$$

Estimated product

$$\begin{array}{r} 20 \\ \times 5 \\ \hline \end{array}$$

Note: Do not round single-digit numbers.

The estimated product is _____ the exact product.

Rounding Numbers
Head for Home Math, Grade 4

Rounding Number to Compare Answers

Directions: Read each problem carefully. Circle the letter of the correct answer. For the open-ended items, write or draw your answer in the space provided.

1 Round the numbers to the nearest ten and estimate the sum. Which problem has an estimate that is more than the exact sum?

A. 36
   15
  + 18

B. 22
   14
  + 19

C. 11
   12
  + 18

D. 34
   42
  + 17

2 Which of these problems has an estimated sum greater than the exact sum?

A. 21
   36
  + 45

B. 63
   54
  + 19

C. 12
   81
  + 23

D. 34
   28
  + 53

3 Which of these problems has an estimated product less than the exact product?

A. 16
  × 6

B. 27
  × 4

C. 32
  × 5

D. 45
  × 3

4 Round the numbers to the nearest ten and estimate the difference. Which problem has an estimate that is greater than the exact difference?

A. 33
        −12

B. 56
        −21

C. 72
        −56

D. 94
        −32

5 Round the numbers to the nearest ten and estimate the product. Which problem has an estimate that is less than the exact product?

A. 27
        × 5

B. 32
        × 2

C. 55
        × 3

D. 76
        × 4

6 Find the estimated difference.

   84
  −25

7 Round the numbers 92 and 21 to the nearest tens. Then subtract the rounded numbers to estimate the difference. Which statement is true?

   A. The estimate is greater the exact difference.

   B. The estimate is less than the exact difference.

   C. The estimate is the same as the exact difference.

   D. The exact answer is half of the estimate.

8 Round the number 28 to the nearest ten. Multiply the rounded number by 4 to estimate the product. Which statement is true?

   A. The estimate is greater than the exact product.

   B. The estimate is less than the exact product.

   C. The estimate is the same as the exact product.

   D. The exact answer is greater than the estimate by 32.

9 Round the numbers 59 and 28 to the nearest tens. Add the rounded numbers to estimate the sum. Which statement is true?

   A. The estimate is greater than the exact sum.

   B. The estimate is less than the exact sum.

   C. The estimate is the same as the exact sum.

   D. The exact answer is more than 10 less than the estimate.

10 Round the numbers 43 and 91 to the nearest tens. Find the estimated sum. Is the estimated sum greater or less than the exact sum?

11 For each problem, round the numbers to the nearest ten and estimate the sum. Which problem has an estimate that is greater than the exact sum?

A. 24
  33
+ 12

B. 46
  57
+ 18

C. 51
  42
+ 33

D. 14
  53
+ 32

12 For each problem, round the numbers to the nearest ten and estimate the difference. Which problem has an estimate that is more than the exact difference?

A. 78
− 13

B. 84
− 62

C. 54
− 23

D. 29
− 18

13 Write the estimated and exact sums for this problem. Then write if the estimated sum is greater than or less than the exact sum.

  14
  15
+ 16

Estimated sum: _____ Exact sum: _____

Which is greater? _____

14 Write the estimated and exact difference for this problem. Then write if the estimated difference is greater than or less than the exact difference.

  84
− 22

Estimated sum: _____ Exact sum: _____

Which is greater? _____

Skill Focus: Converting Metric Units

Objective: To convert from one measurement unit to another using unit equivalencies within the metric measuring system

The **metric system** is a system of measurement based on tens. Units of measure in the metric system include centimeter, meter, kilometer, gram, kilogram, milliliter, and liter.

A **centimeter (cm)** is a unit of length in the metric system. The width of a paper clip is about 1 cm.

A **kilometer (km)** is a unit of length in the metric system. A 5-kilometer race is the same as a 3.1-mile race.

A **liter (L)** is a unit of capacity in the metric system. A large bottle of soda is 2 L.

A **milliliter (mL)** is a unit of capacity in the metric system. A liter is equal to 1,000 milliliters.

A **meter (m)** is a unit of length in the metric system. A refrigerator is a little less than 2 meters tall.

Follow the steps below to convert units of measure in the metric system.

Metric Conversions

Length	1 kilometer (km) = 1,000 meters (m)
	1 meter (m) = 100 centimeters (cm)
Capacity	1 liter (L) = 1,000 milliliters (mL)

Multiply or Divide?

Conversion Direction	Operation
Larger units to smaller units	multiply
Smaller units to larger units	divide

Step 1: Decide if you are converting from a larger unit to a smaller one or a smaller unit to a larger one.

Step 2: Then determine which operation you will use.

Step 3: Use that operation with the proper metric conversion.

Example: It is 8 **kilometers** from the neighborhood park to the city library. How many **meters** is it from the park to the library?

You are converting kilometers to meters, so you are converting from a larger unit to a smaller one.

You will need to multiply.

Multiply: 8 kilometers by 1,000 because every kilometer = 1,000 meters

$$8 \times 1,000 = 8,000 \text{ meters}$$

Converting Metric Units

Directions: Read each problem carefully. Circle the letter of the correct answer. For the open-ended items, write or draw your answer in the space provided.

1 The slide is 3 meters high, which is _____ centimeters tall.

2 Five liters of milk is _____ milliliters.

3 The bus traveled 22 kilometers, which is _____ meters.

4 Four thousand milliliters of orange juice is _____ liters.

5 The distance between the lakes is 49,000 meters, which is _____ kilometers.

6 Tarek wants to find out how many milliliters are in a 2-liter bottle of iced tea. Explain how Tarek can find the answer.

_____

_____

_____

7 Shannon ran a 5-kilometer race. How many meters did Shannon run?

A. 1,000 meters   **B.** 3,000 meters

C. 5,000 meters   **D.** 10,000 meters

8 Sam bought a 1-liter bottle of juice for the party. How many milliliters of juice does the bottle contain?

A. 1,000 milliliters   **B.** 500 milliliters

C. 100 milliliters   **D.** 10 milliliters

9 The height of the classroom door is 3 meters. How tall is the classroom door in centimeters?

A. 30 centimeters

B. 300 centimeters

C. 3,000 centimeters

D. 6,000 centimeters

10 Mark went on a 7-kilometer hike. How many meters did Mark hike?

A. 7,000 meters

B. 700 meters

C. 70 meters

D. 7 meters

11 Susan measured her bedroom wall, and it was 5 meters long. How many centimeters long was the wall?

A. 50 centimeters

B. 100 centimeters

C. 200 centimeters

D. 500 centimeters

12 Becky emptied 4,000 milliliters of dirty water from her fish tank. How many liters of water did Becky empty?

A. 4 liters

B. 8 liters

C. 40 liters

D. 400 liters

Converting Metric Units
Head for Home Math, Grade 4

13 Justin is 200 centimeters tall. How tall is Justin in meters? Explain your reasoning.

_____

_____

_____

14 Jerry and Connor biked to Gavin's house, which was 6,000 meters from their house. How many kilometers did Jerry and Connor ride?

A. 1 kilometers

B. 2 kilometers

C. 6 kilometers

D. 9 kilometers

15 Mr. Kline measured the length of his new car to make sure it would fit in his garage, and it was 3.5 meters long. How long is Mr. Kline's car in centimeters?

A. 300 centimeters

B. 350 centimeters

C. 3,000 centimeters

D. 3,500 centimeters

16 Lana collected 3,000 milliliters of rainwater in a bucket for her science project. How many liter bottles will she need to bring the rainwater to school? Explain your reasoning.

_____

_____

_____

Answer Key

Associative Property of Multiplication, pp. 3–8
Example 1: 40
Example 2: 6, 30; 15, 30

Multiplying Using the Associative Property, pp. 5–8
1. B
2. A
3. D
4. 3 × (5 × 4); (3 × 4) × 5
5. C
6. C
7. D
8. C
9. C
10. A
11. B
12. Andrew did not regroup the factors and he changed a multiplication sign to a plus sign.
13. They will both get the same answer. The Associative Property of Multiplication says you can multiply in any order and will get the same answer.
14. 4
15. 4 × (9 × 2)

Remainders, pp. 9–14
Example: 33 − 30 = 3; 6 r3

Dividing with Remainders, pp. 11–14
1. 2 r1
2. 2; 1; 2 r1
3. Check children's drawings to make sure they have drawn 13 objects in 6 groups of 2 objects, with 1 left over.
4. 3; 2; 3 r2
5. B
6. 18 ÷ 6 = 3; 23 − 18 = 5; 23 ÷ 6 = 3 r5
7. C
8. A
9. D
10. Michael did not use the nearest fact that was less than the dividend, he used the nearest fact that was greater. He should use 20 ÷ 4 = 5
11. D
12. Check work. 6 r2
13. Check work. 7 r1
14. Check work. 3 r1

Numbers and Place Value, pp. 15–20

Example 2: nine thousand four hundred thirty-two

Example 4: 7,062

Example 5: four thousand, one hundred seven

Example 2: 3; 5; 1

Example 3: 9 thousands; 5 hundreds

Writing Numbers and Determining Values, pp. 18–20

1. C
2. D
3. C
4. 4
5. A
6. A
7. D
8. B
9. 8,007
10. B
11. 6 thousands or 6,000; 1 ten or 10; 2 ones
12. nine thousand, four hundred eight

Adding Fractions, pp. 21–26

Example 2: $7\frac{2}{3}$

Example 3: 6

Adding Fractions and Mixed Numbers, pp. 24–25

1. $\frac{7}{10}$; 7 parts should be shaded
2. $\frac{1+2}{9} = \frac{3}{9} = \frac{1}{3}$
3. C
4. B
5. C

Adding Mixed Numbers, pp. 25–26

6. D
7. A

8. D
9. C
10. $9\frac{2}{5}$

Subtracting Fractions, pp. 27–32

Example 2: $1\frac{1}{9}$

Subtracting Fractions, pp. 29–30

1. $\frac{1}{3}$; Cross out 3 sections
2. $\frac{8-3}{10} = \frac{5}{10} = \frac{1}{2}$
3. B
4. A
5. D
6. D

Subtracting Mixed Numbers, pp. 31–32

7. B
8. C
9. A
10. C
11. $2\frac{5}{12}$

Decimals, pp. 33–38

Practicing Decimal Number Place Value, pp. 35–38

1. 25 squares should be shaded
2. 9 squares should be shaded
3. 8 sections should be shaded
4. six hundred seventy-eight thousandths
5. thirty-two hundredths
6. eighty hundredths or eight tenths
7. C
8. D
9. B
10. C
11. D
12. A

Number Patterns, pp. 39–43

Example 1: 8
Example 2: 32; multiply by 2
Example: 24, 6

Using Patterns, pp. 41–43

1. C
2. A
3. C
4. D
5. B
6. A
7. A
8. C
9. 34; add 2
10. 3; subtract 3
11. 47; add 5, subtract 1
12. 16; 29; add 6, subtract 1

Equations, pp. 44–49

Working with Equations, pp. 46–49

1. D
2. C
3. A
4. $b - 34 = 23$
5. B
6. C
7. Check work; $j = 40$
8. B
9. Check work; 11
10. A
11. D
12. Check work; $c - 13 = 23$; 36

Rounding Numbers, pp. 50–55

Example 1: greater than
Example 2: 80; 100; greater than

Rounding Number to Compare Answers, pp. 52–55

1. A
2. A
3. C
4. B
5. B
6. 50
7. B
8. A
9. A
10. 130; less than
11. B
12. A
13. exact 45; estimated 50, estimated sum is greater than exact sum
14. exact 62; estimated 60, estimated difference is less than exact difference

Converting Metric Units, pp. 56–60

Converting Metric Units, pp. 58–60

1. 300
2. 5,000
3. 22,000
4. 4
5. 49
6. Tarek needs to multiply 2 (for the 2 liters) by 1,000 (for the 1,000 milliliters in a liter) to find that there are 2,000 milliliters in the 2-liter bottle.
7. C
8. A
9. B
10. A
11. D
12. A
13. 2 meters; divide 200 by 100 because there are 100 centimeters in 1 meter
14. C
15. B
16. 3 bottles. 1 liter equals 1,000 milliliters, so she will need 3 1-liter bottles.